Contents

		page
Introduction		v
Chapter 1	The Great Wind	1
Chapter 2	The Island	5
Chapter 3	Five Again	7
Chapter 4	The Box	10
Chapter 5	The Rock Wall	12
Chapter 6	Inside the Rock	14
Chapter 7	Cave House	17
Chapter 8	Visitors	21
Chapter 9	Answers	25
Chapter 10	The Mysterious Helper	27
Chapter 11	Below the Cave Floor	29
Chapter 12	Last Words	31
Chapter 13	Smoke!	34
Activities		37

Introduction

The balloon came down quickly now and the great waves tried to catch them.

Then Cyrus Smith fell into the sea. Did he fall or did he jump? Top, the dog, saw his master in the water and jumped in after him.

There are four men, a boy and a dog in a balloon over the Pacific, but only three men and the boy arrive on a strange island. Will they find Cyrus and Top again? Are there other people on the island? Why do strange things happen to them there? And will they see their homes again?

Jules Verne was born in Nantes, in the west of France, in 1828. The 1800s were a time of exciting ideas – people built trains, balloons and submarines. When he was a young man, Jules Verne loved new ideas. There are a lot of them in his stories. He also loved journeys round the world, and he loved the sea. When he was a boy, he tried to run away to sea.

Jules Verne wrote *Five Weeks in a Balloon*, his first book about an exciting journey, in 1862. Everybody in France loved it and it came out in English in 1869. He then wrote other stories: *Journey to the Centre of the Earth, From the Earth to the Moon* (a journey of 97 hours and 20 minutes!), *Twenty Thousand Leagues under the Sea* (about Captain Nemo and his submarine, *Nautilus*) and his most famous book, *Round the World in Eighty Days* (also in Penguin Readers). He wrote *The Mysterious Island* in 1874–5.

Jules Verne made a lot of money from his books and he bought a boat. He made journeys round the world and wrote at the same time. Then in 1896 he sold his boat. His eyes were weak and he stopped writing. He died in 1905.

Chapter 1   The Great Wind

One day, in March 1865, there was a great wind. It began quite suddenly. It pulled down trees and buildings across the world. It sent many ships to the bottom of the sea.

When the wind began, there were four men, a boy and a dog high in the sky in a balloon. How did they get there?

In America in 1865, there was fighting between the north of the country and the south. These four men were prisoners in the town of Richmond, Virginia, in the south. One day they took a balloon – but that's a different story! They flew north in the balloon. A boy helped them to get away, and they took him with them. One man had a dog, and they took him, too.

But they took the balloon on the wrong day. They took it on that day in March, 1865, the day of the great wind.

◆

The wind caught the balloon and carried it away from the land and out over the Pacific. The balloon went faster and faster. The wind pushed it this way and that way.

After many days, the wind got weaker, but then the balloon started to go down. It fell very, very quickly. The men shouted, 'Throw out more bags!'

'That's the last bag.'

'Are we going up again?'

'No, we're going down.'

'Look! We're near the sea!'

'Look at the waves. They're thirty feet high. We'll die. What can we do?'

'Throw everything out,' shouted one man.

They flew north in the balloon.

He was strong and he was not afraid. His name was Cyrus Smith.

They threw everything out – guns, food, water, money. The boy had the dog in his arms.

The balloon climbed into the sky. For a long time the balloon stayed up and moved south. Then it began to go down again. They could not see land anywhere. The great waves came nearer and nearer.

'Everybody climb up onto the ropes,' shouted Cyrus Smith.

The four men and the boy climbed up the ropes. The boy carried the dog. Then they cut the ropes and everything below them fell into the sea. Slowly the balloon began to go up.

Suddenly one of the men shouted, 'Land!'

It was Pencroft. Pencroft was a seaman and his eyes were good.

After some minutes, the other men could see land, too. A long way away. Dark grey mountains. Slowly the land got nearer, and the grey turned to green. They could see yellow beaches.

The balloon came down quickly now and the great waves tried to catch them.

Then Cyrus Smith fell into the sea. Did he fall or did he jump? Top, the dog, saw his master in the water and jumped in after him.

'No!' cried the boy.

But the balloon climbed up again and took them slowly away.

Now they were near land and they could not see Cyrus or his dog. The balloon flew down over a beach and the three men and the boy jumped to the ground. The wind caught the balloon and took it away into the sky. They ran back to the sea.

'Can anybody see Cyrus?' asked one man. 'Let's stay here and wait.'

His name was Gideon Spillet, and he worked for a newspaper, the *New York Herald*.

'We can't stay here,' said Pencroft. 'This is a very small island, and there's nothing here. There's no water and there are no trees. The next island is much bigger and has mountains. The sea will carry Mr Smith there.'

Nab, the third man, ran quickly into the sea and began to swim. He was on his way to the big island. Nab was Cyrus Smith's man and he loved his master.

Chapter 2   The Island

The others could all swim, but Nab was the fastest. When he got to the beach, he started to look for Cyrus Smith. He couldn't wait.

'There are a lot of trees,' said Spillet to the other man and the boy. 'And perhaps we can find water in those mountains. I want to climb up high and look at the island. Perhaps there are people here. Will you two go that way, down the beach, and look for food and water? Let's meet here again before the sun goes down.'

Pencroft and Herbert, the boy, walked down the beach to the south. They came to some rocks. They climbed up into the rocks and found a cave. There was a little river near it.

'This is a good place for us. There's water, and food in the rocks,' said Pencroft.

'Food?' asked Herbert. 'I can see a cave and water, but where's the food?'

'There'll be fish round the rocks.'

'But we have to cook the fish first. And we haven't got a fire.'

Pencroft felt in his coat, but his box of matches wasn't there.

'Perhaps one of the other men has some matches,' he said. 'Let's go and find wood for a fire. Then we'll put branches across the mouth of the cave.'

They jumped over the little river and went into the trees behind the cave.

'Mr Pencroft!' shouted Herbert suddenly. 'There are some eggs here.'

They took the eggs, some dead wood and some green branches back to the cave.

◆

When Pencroft and Herbert arrived back at the beach, they found Spillet and Nab there. Spillet looked very tired. Nab's eyes were red. He sat down and looked out at the sea.

'I climbed to the highest place on the island,' said Spillet. 'I couldn't see any sign of life. And Nab didn't find any sign of Cyrus or Top on the island.'

They all felt sad.

Chapter 3   Five Again

Spillet found one match in his coat.

'Let's be careful here,' said Pencroft. 'We can light a fire now, so that's good. But we'll have to watch it. It can't go out.'

They ate a wonderful dinner of eggs and fish. After dinner, Herbert went to sleep. Spillet wrote in his notebook. Then he, too, tried to sleep. Pencroft woke every hour and put more wood on the fire. Nab didn't try to sleep. He walked up and down the beach all night.

◆

Before it was light, the sound of feet woke them. Nab and Top, the dog, stood in the mouth of the cave.

'Look! Top's here!' said Nab, and he smiled for the first time.

Top looked at the men and the boy. He barked excitedly. He ran out of the cave and in again. He ran from one person to the next person. He barked and barked.

'Top wants us to follow him,' said Nab. 'Perhaps he wants to take us to Mr Smith. Let's go.'

And at that minute, the sun came up over the sea. It washed the island in red light.

'How did the dog find us?' thought Spillet. 'He doesn't know his way round the island. He isn't tired. It's very mysterious.'

They followed Top. He stayed on the beach for about three miles. Then he turned away from the sea and ran up into the mountains. He started to get excited and barked loudly. They came to another cave and Top ran in. They all followed.

They found Cyrus Smith on the floor of the cave. His eyes were closed. He didn't move when his friends called his name.

'NO!' cried Nab. 'He's dead!'

'Ssh!' said Spillet. He got down next to Cyrus and listened.

He put his hand over Cyrus's mouth.

'No,' he said after a minute. 'He isn't dead, but he's very weak. Get some water quickly.'

They put some water into his mouth. They put their coats over him and made him warm. They held his hands and talked quietly to him. After some time, Spillet listened again.

'He's a little stronger. I think he's going to live.'

They sat with Cyrus. They watched him carefully and gave him little drinks of water. About three hours later, Cyrus opened his eyes.

'Where am I?' he asked weakly.

'We think we're on a large island,' said Spillet. 'And there are smaller islands near here. We have water, a good cave near the beach and firewood. We can't find any sign of other people on the islands.'

'Is Pencroft here too? And Herbert and Nab?'

'We're all here, master,' said Nab happily, and Top barked.

Cyrus slept again for many hours. When he woke up, he felt stronger.

'How did I get to this place?' he asked. 'I remember some things. Top and I swam to land and then a great wave threw us onto the beach. But nothing after that. Is this cave near the sea? I can't hear the waves.'

'It's more than half a mile to the sea from here,' said Pencroft.

'Then somebody carried me.'

'*We* didn't carry you,' said Spillet. 'And there are no other people on the island. Perhaps you walked here but you can't remember.'

'But I was tired and very weak.'

With one arm round Nab and the other round Pencroft, Cyrus Smith stood up and walked to the mouth of the cave. They looked at the ground. In one place it was wet and there were signs – signs of a man's shoes.

'Nobody here is wearing these shoes,' said Cyrus. 'And my shoes are in the sea.'

'It's very mysterious,' said Spillet.

◆

It was a long, slow journey back to the cave near the beach. They carried Cyrus. The sky was black when they arrived. They were tired and hungry. Cyrus ate an egg and then fell asleep on a comfortable bed of young branches.

Chapter 4   The Box

'What can we eat?' asked Cyrus the next morning.

'Eggs or fish,' answered Pencroft.

'Where do the eggs come from?'

'I found them on the ground,' said Herbert. 'There were about twenty eggs in one place.'

'Then we can also eat birds. And fruit from the trees.'

'How are we going to catch birds?' asked Herbert. 'We threw the guns out of the balloon. I threw rocks at some birds yesterday, but I couldn't hit them.'

'We'll make bows,' Spillet said.

Pencroft found some wood and he started to make a bow with his knife.

They now had to learn to use their bows. Spillet and Herbert were the best bowmen and birds were often on the dinner table after that.

They cooked their food over an open fire. And they always watched the fire – it never went out.

'We're doing well,' said Spillet, after the first days, 'but what other things will make life easier for us? Let's think, and I'll write them in my notebook.'

That evening they all thought of things for their life on the island. Spillet wrote them down.

◆

Often the sea washed things onto the island. Every day they looked on the beach, in the rocks and in the wood. One man always stayed at the cave and watched the fire. Every day one man climbed to the highest place on the island and looked for signs of life – ships at sea or people on the land.

One day, about a month after the great wind, they went

south down the beach from their cave. They left Spillet at the fire. Herbert ran in front of the men. Then he came back and shouted excitedly, 'Come and see! Come and see!'

And there, on the beach, was a big box.

'Did this come from a ship?' asked Cyrus Smith. 'It's very heavy. Why didn't it go to the bottom of the sea?'

'Let's open it and look inside,' said Herbert. He jumped up and down. Top barked loudly.

There were ropes round the box, and they were wet from the sea. Pencroft cut them with his knife. Then Herbert opened the box.

Inside, the box was dry.

'Is this really happening?' said Pencroft.

They looked into the box, and their eyes and mouths opened wide.

Everything from Spillet's notebook was there. Now they could cook, fish, write, fight and build. There were clothes in the box, too, and some coffee.

They carried the heavy box back to their cave and showed everything to Spillet.

'It's very mysterious,' said Cyrus Smith.

'There are a lot of mysterious things round here,' said Spillet.

'But who put these things into the box? And why?' asked Cyrus. Nobody had any answers.

They had a good dinner that evening. They made coffee and talked for a long time.

Chapter 5   The Rock Wall

The next morning the four men and the boy took food, knives, guns, matches and rope from the box. They left the other things and put the ropes round it again. They put the box on a high rock shelf. Nobody could see it from the mouth of the cave.

They went south down the beach again. This time they all went. Nobody had to stay with the fire now, because they had matches. The fire could go out for the first time.

The sun shone and there was a warm wind. They enjoyed the beautiful Pacific colours – yellow beaches, light green trees, blue-green water, light blue sky.

After about half a mile, the land changed. The beach here was only about three feet wide. Tall trees came down to the sea. Behind the trees there was a high wall of rock.

'You can see this rock wall from the highest place,' said Spillet. 'It's a wall but it's almost half a mile thick. Behind it there's a wide river. The river starts high in the mountains over there.'

'Where does the river come out?' asked Cyrus.

'Let's go and see,' said Herbert.

They walked through the trees and climbed round the end of the rock wall. It was a difficult climb, but then they came to the river. It was very slow and wide here. They were hungry now and Pencroft and Nab tried to catch some fish.

'The water is very warm here,' said Pencroft. 'The fish are at the bottom in the colder water.'

'The river is moving that way,' said Nab.

They all looked at the thick trees at the bottom of the rock wall.

That night they slept next to the water at the foot of the rock wall. The next morning they made their way round the river. Cyrus Smith went first. The other people followed him through the thick trees. They could hear the sound of water. It got louder and louder. Then they came to an open place in the trees.

They stood and looked for some minutes. The river ran nearly to the rock wall, and then went into the ground below.

Cyrus Smith looked round him, and then looked up at the rock wall. There was a big cave about thirty feet above them.

'Look up at that cave,' said Cyrus. 'In past times the river went out through the rock wall there. The water was higher then. Now it goes through the ground to the sea. I want to look in that cave.'

'It'll be dark in there,' said Pencroft. 'Nab and I will look for branches. Then we can make lights.'

Chapter 6   Inside the Rock

The mouth of the cave in the rock wall was about twenty feet wide, but only three feet high. Nab and Pencroft broke some rock away so they could get in.

Cyrus Smith lit a branch and went in. The way through the rock was only six feet high and three feet wide. It was cold and wet and they had to move carefully. They went slowly down. After a time, it opened into a long, wide cave and they could move faster. Cyrus stopped them.

'Let's use the rope. Then nobody will fall.' He called to Top. 'You go first, boy.'

'We're going down to the sea,' said Cyrus.

They turned to the right and suddenly stopped. They were at the mouth of a great underground cave.

Nab and Pencroft moved their branches above their heads and the light got stronger. Cyrus and Spillet stood ready with their guns. Pencroft had his knife. There was nothing in the cave. At the opposite end there was some light from outside.

'Let's go to that light,' said Cyrus. 'I think it comes from the front of the rock wall – near the sea. Watch your feet. Top, go in front of us.'

Top started to run to the opposite end. Before he got there, he stopped. He barked loudly. The other men followed carefully. The floor of the cave opened in front of them. It went down a long way and they could not see the bottom. Cyrus found a small rock and threw it down.

'One, two, three . . . sixteen, seventeen, eighteen.'

Then the rock hit the water below.

'About a hundred feet,' said Cyrus. 'That's the sea down there. We're about a hundred feet above the sea here. Let's find our way round this.'

The floor of the cave opened in front of them.

They came to the light at the end of the cave.

'The rock's thinner here,' said Pencroft. 'I'll try to break more away.'

He worked hard. When he was tired, Nab worked at it. Then Spillet. Suddenly, the rock fell away and light came in. They looked round. The great cave was clean and dry. A small river ran through it.

'Good water,' said Pencroft. 'We can drink this.'

'Let's make more windows,' said Herbert. 'Then we can live here. This cave's a wonderful place.'

'But first we have to get out again through the dark rock,' said Pencroft, 'and the light from our branches is going.'

They started on their journey back up through the rock. The last branch went out minutes after they arrived in the outside world.

'We'll have to sleep here another night,' said Cyrus.

But it wasn't a good night and they didn't sleep. There was a great wind and heavy rain. Branches fell from the trees. The rain ran down the rock wall in rivers.

Chapter 7   Cave House

When it was light, the four men, the boy and the dog – cold, wet and tired – began their difficult journey back to their cave near the beach. The warm sun shone and their clothes were quickly dry. The ground was very wet and the rivers were very high.

After a long time, they got back to the beach. The wind was quiet now, but great waves washed onto the land.

'Look!' said Cyrus. 'The sea came over the beach and the rocks in the night. Our cave will be very wet.'

'I hope the box is all right,' said Herbert.

They arrived back at the beach cave in the afternoon. The floor was wet and their beds and fireplace were not there. But the big box was fine on its shelf. They opened it and it was dry inside.

Again they felt strange. Did somebody watch over them in the night?

'We'll have to move higher up,' said Cyrus, 'before that wind comes back.'

'Let's go to the great cave in the rock wall,' said Herbert.

'We can go there, but . . .' said Cyrus.

'But what?' said Pencroft. He liked the idea.

Cyrus said, 'We can't use the long way in and out every time. We'll have to find another way.'

'Perhaps there's a way in from the front,' said Spillet.

'Hmm,' said Cyrus. 'I looked at it from the beach on the way back. Our window is about eighty feet up the rock wall from the ground.' He turned to Pencroft. 'Can we climb up there with ropes?'

'Yes,' said Pencroft. 'But a very long rope will be dangerous in a high wind. There's a shelf in the rock, halfway up. We can use two shorter forty foot ropes.'

'Have we got eighty feet of rope?' asked Spillet.

'I can make rope,' said Pencroft. 'Everything for that is here on the island.'

◆

It was a week before they moved into their new home. 'Cave House', they called it. They made more windows. Pencroft and Spillet made ropes. Herbert and Nab made beds, chairs and tables out of wood. They pulled them up into the cave house on the ropes. Cyrus made a fireplace, and shelves on the walls of the cave. They broke through the rock above the fire.

'Now the smoke can get out,' said Cyrus.

They thought about possible problems and they tried to think of answers.

'When we're all in Cave House,' said Cyrus, 'we can pull up the ropes. Nobody can get to us then.'

'We'll always have to have food for three or four days in the cave,' said Spillet. 'There'll be times when we can't go out for fruit or eggs or fish.'

They worked hard and each person learned about the other people. There were never any angry words. They were good friends.

Herbert did very well. He planned and built things very carefully. He was a quick learner. Pencroft and Nab taught him a lot of things. He learned to make ropes and catch fish. He learned to build with wood. Spillet helped him to read and write. Cyrus taught him the story of America and about places round the world. And he talked to him about ideas. Herbert wasn't a child and he wasn't a man. But he worked as hard as the older men.

Pencroft liked Cyrus Smith. He was wonderful, he thought. He was not afraid of him and he listened carefully to his words. In the evenings Pencroft often told stories about his life at sea. Did his stories really happen? It wasn't important – they were

They were good friends.

good stories. Herbert and Nab enjoyed them. Pencroft was very clever with his hands, too.

Nab was Nab. He always helped everybody. And for his master, he was ready to die. He was clever, too. When they had a problem, Nab always had a good idea. And he was a fine cook.

They all liked Gideon Spillet. 'He's a writer,' Pencroft said to Nab, 'a newspaper man. He knows things and he understands things. But he can do things too. He can use his head *and* his hands.'

Chapter 8 Visitors

Cyrus Smith said, 'We have to watch for ships. Let's have one man at the cave window all day and all night.'

One evening some time later, Herbert was at the window.

'A ship! A ship!' he cried.

Top barked loudly. Pencroft quickly put out the fire.

They had a plan.

'Is it coming this way?' Cyrus asked Pencroft.

'I don't know,' said Pencroft. 'Let's wait.'

The ship came nearer, but it was quite dark. Pencroft looked very hard.

'It isn't American ... or British ... or French ...' Then he could see. 'Pirates!' he cried.

A lot of questions went through Cyrus Smith's head. What did pirates want here? There were no people. There was nothing.

'Listen, my friends,' he said. 'Perhaps they're only looking at the island. Perhaps they won't get off their ship. But we don't want to show any sign of us or our cave house.'

Everybody worked quickly. Pencroft pulled up the ropes. Nab and Spillet put branches across the cave windows. Herbert took Top down to the back of the cave. Smith watched.

The pirate ship came in near the beach. The men in the cave could only wait. Night came.

'They're staying,' said Pencroft. 'They'll come to the island in small boats in the morning.'

'Let's hope they only want water,' said Cyrus. 'Let's hope they leave quickly.'

'I think I'll go out there,' said Pencroft.

'What do you mean?' asked Herbert.

'I'll swim to their ship.'

'You're a good man,' said Spillet.

Pencroft opened his knife and put it between his teeth. He climbed quickly down the ropes. Then he went quietly through the trees to the beach and swam out to the ship. It was a black night. The lights of the ship showed him the way. Pencroft swam to one of the ship's ropes. Some men stood near him on the ship. He listened.

'This is a good ship,' said one man.

'Yes, and we took it easily! But we had to kill the women too – that was bad.'

'Yes, I wanted one of those women,' said a third man.

'But it's better that way. First, we can have a good time. Then we have to kill them. We don't want anybody to talk.'

'That's right – the boss knows best.'

'Bob Harvey – the most famous pirate on the sea!'

Bob Harvey! Pencroft knew that name. He was the most famous and the most dangerous pirate. Many years before, Harvey and his men were prisoners in Australia. But they got away. Nobody could catch them.

The men laughed and drank. They talked about the women on ships and on these quiet and beautiful Pacific islands. Pencroft hated listening to them.

'What can we do?' he thought. 'How many pirates are there and how many guns do they have?'

He waited in the cold water. The lights on the ship went out. The men were asleep. There was nobody outside. Pencroft climbed up and went quietly round the ship. He saw about fifty men and four big guns.

'They can easily hit the rock wall from here with these guns,' he thought.

He knew everything now, and he swam quickly back to land.

At Cave House, Pencroft told his story.

'There are five of us and fifty of them,' he said.

Pencroft swam to one of the ship's ropes.

The next morning they saw the pirates on the ship. The ship came in nearer to the beach. Suddenly they heard the sound of a big gun. The pirates wanted to hit the rocks.

'They don't know we're here,' said Pencroft. 'They always do this before they send their boats to land.'

Again there was the sound of a gun. This time it hit the rock wall high up near their cave. The floor and walls of the cave moved. Some branches fell away from a window and smoke came into the cave.

'That's bad,' said Pencroft. 'Bob Harvey isn't stupid. He'll see the window and turn his guns to it.'

'Yes,' said Cyrus. 'Stand away from it. Now the pirates know we're here. We'll be prisoners in our cave.'

At that minute there was a loud noise and a great light outside followed by cries from the men on the ship. The five friends forgot Cyrus's words and ran to the window. A great wall of water carried the pirate ship up and up. Then the wave broke and hit the ship.

There was smoke everywhere. The two halves of the ship fell back and went down to the bottom of the sea. Great waves washed onto the beach. Now they could see only the top of the ship above the water.

Chapter 9   Answers

'Quickly!' shouted Cyrus Smith. 'Come down to the beach, and bring your guns with you! Perhaps some pirates weren't on the ship.'

The sea was quiet now. They could see the ship on the bottom. Most pirates were inside the ship, but some men were in the water. The four men and the boy pulled them out, but they were dead.

'We'll have to wait,' said Pencroft. 'When the sea goes out, we can swim down to the ship. But what happened to it? What do you think, Mr Smith?'

'And why did it happen at the right time?' said Spillet.

'I don't know. It's very mysterious,' said Cyrus. 'Perhaps we'll find the answers at the bottom of the sea.'

Some hours later, Pencroft and Nab swam to the ship. The bottom of the ship was in two halves.

They swam to the ship many times over the next two days. They found clothes and shoes, guns and food. But then another great wind came and the ship broke again. The wind and the waves washed it out to sea.

'Now we'll never know the answer to the big question – what really happened to that ship?' said Cyrus. 'I don't think it hit rocks.'

'No, it didn't,' said Pencroft. 'There aren't any rocks there. And we all saw the ship on a wall of water.'

'You're right,' said Cyrus.

◆

Some days later, Nab found something strange on the beach. He took it back to Cyrus at the cave house. Cyrus looked at it carefully.

'Nab,' he said, 'this is the answer to our big question. But it leaves us with a bigger question.'

He showed it to the other men. Spillet took it and turned it in his hands.

'This is very interesting!' he said, and he looked at Cyrus. 'And it's very mysterious!'

'What's it from?' said Herbert.

'It's from a torpedo,' said Spillet.

Chapter 10   The Mysterious Helper

'So the question now is: where did a torpedo come from in the middle of the Pacific?' said Cyrus. 'We aren't the only people on this island. Somebody's here with us. Somebody's helping us. Let's think about the signs. One: They carried me from the beach to a cave. Two: They gave us the big box and everything in it. Three: They killed the pirates—'

'With a torpedo,' said Spillet.

'With a torpedo. Four: Top knows there's somebody on the island. He often barks at nothing – but *is* it nothing?'

Nab spoke. 'We won't see this person before they're ready.'

◆

Then their mysterious friend helped them again.

Herbert suddenly got ill. When he was hot, Cyrus and the other men washed him with cold water. When he was cold, they put him by the fire. Everybody was very sad. Herbert was really ill and they couldn't help him.

At three o'clock one morning, Nab made a cold drink for him. The other men were asleep. Suddenly Top barked loudly. Nab ran back to Herbert. When he got there, Top was quiet. But on the table next to Herbert's bed was a bottle. Nab quickly called Cyrus Smith.

Cyrus opened the bottle. He tried it and then gave it to Herbert.

'Now Herbert will get better,' he said.

Slowly Herbert got stronger and stronger. In two weeks he was fine.

◆

Months later there was no sign from their friend. Then one morning when they came back to the cave, Top was very excited.

He barked and barked and ran round the table.

'Did we have a visitor, Top?' asked Cyrus.

There was a note on the table. It said: 'Now *I* am dying. Come down through the cave floor. You will find me there.'

Chapter 11   Below the Cave Floor

'We know there's water at the bottom,' said Cyrus. 'It's about a hundred feet down. We want a rope about 200 feet long.'

'I'll go down first,' said Pencroft. 'When I want something, I'll shout.'

He climbed easily and quickly down the rope. He took a branch, some matches and his knife with him.

After some minutes, he shouted up.

'I'm on a shelf of rock next to the water. I can't see very well. But I think I'm in another great big cave. And I think there's water everywhere down here.'

Nab came down next. He brought a light too.

Nab and Pencroft looked round them. The others climbed down.

'Look,' said Pencroft, 'a boat!'

It was under a shelf of rock. When Cyrus saw it, he said, 'We can all get in there. I think somebody left it here for us. Follow me.'

'Now where?' asked Spillet, when they were all sitting in the little boat.

'I don't know,' said Cyrus. 'Is anybody there?' he shouted.

His words flew round the cave and came back to them.

Suddenly a white light lit the cave. It shone across the water. The cave was very big – bigger than their cave house above. And the light? It was very mysterious. The light came from something in the water in the middle of the cave. It was about 250 feet long. Half of it was above the water and half was below the water. The part above the water was about twelve feet high.

'What is it? Is it a ship?' asked Herbert quietly. He was afraid.

Cyrus Smith stood up in the little boat and looked hard at the thing in front of them. Suddenly he took Spillet's arm.

'It's him,' he said quietly in Spillet's ear. And he said a name.

Gideon Spillet's eyes opened wide. 'Him!' he said. 'But isn't he dead?'

Chapter 12   Last Words

Pencroft brought the little boat next to the 'ship'. They climbed through a door and went down some stairs. Strong light lit the inside. They came to a heavy door. Cyrus opened it and they went into a large room. There were famous pictures and beautiful things in the room.

An old man sat in a large chair. He did not look at them.

Everybody jumped when Cyrus Smith said loudly, 'Captain Nemo! You invited us here. Here we are.'

The old man stood up slowly. He was ill and weak, but he spoke strongly.

'I did not give you my name, sir.'

'No, but I know you,' Smith answered. 'And I know that this is your submarine, *Nautilus*.'

An angry look moved across Captain Nemo's face. Then he fell back into his chair.

'All right,' he said. 'I am an old man and I am dying. You know only bad stories about me.'

'That isn't important. We know that you're very good to us. You help us all the time.'

'You are good people. You work hard and you are strong,' said the old man. 'Please sit down. I will tell you my story.

'I am an Indian. My name is Prince Dakkar. When I was ten years old, my father sent me to Europe. I studied there for many years. I was another rich young Asian student. But I studied hard because I hated the British. The British took India from the Indians – I wanted it for my people.

'Then something happened. In 1857, the Indians fought the British. I fought with them. We waited for help from outside the country. No help came. My men and I fought hard. I wanted to die for my country. But we did not win. When the last Indian

An old man sat in a large chair.

fighters fell, I had to leave the country.

'Other clever men had to leave, too. I planned and built this submarine. Then those men came with me. We did a lot of things in *Nautilus* — you know that from the newspapers. But when I was sixty, most of my friends were dead. I brought *Nautilus* to this island and lived here quietly, away from the world.

'*Nautilus* will never go to sea again. The mouth of this cave fell in at the time of the great wind — when you came to the island.'

Captain Nemo fell back into his chair again, tired and weak.

Cyrus Smith and Gideon Spillet wanted to help him, but they had no answers.

'I will die tonight or tomorrow,' said Captain Nemo. 'I only want one thing. When I am dead, please leave *Nautilus*. Take only this box with you.' He gave Cyrus a large heavy box. 'With this you will all be very rich one day. But I know you will use the money well. I want the other things to go with me when I die.

'When you leave, get into the little boat. Take the boat to the front end of the submarine. There is a little white door. Open it. Then go to the back. There you will find another door. Open that, too. The water will come in and *Nautilus* will go to the bottom of the cave. I want to go down with it.

'Before I die, please eat a last dinner with me. You will find everything over there.'

Chapter 13   Smoke!

They did everything for Captain Nemo. Then they looked back from the rock shelf. *Nautilus* went down slowly, quietly. They climbed their ropes before the light from the submarine went out.

◆

Captain Nemo's little boat was very good for their life on the island. They caught bigger and better fish out at sea from the boat. They visited the other islands and found different fruits and trees there. They worked hard for two years.

They watched for ships all day and all night, but no ship came near the island. Before he died, Captain Nemo told them something important. The island was not on maps of the Pacific. To the outside world, there *was* no island. They watched and watched. But they never saw anything.

They started to build a ship. Perhaps they could go back to America in that.

One day, Herbert shouted from the cave window,

'Pencroft, my friend with the wonderful eyes, come and look at this! I think I can see smoke!'

Pencroft ran to the window.

'You're right, Herbert. It *is* smoke!'

The smoke came from a ship, and the ship was on its way to the island. They made a great fire on top of the rock wall, with green wood. Thick smoke went up into the sky.

The ship – the *Surveyor* – was British.

'We're making maps of the Pacific Islands,' Captain Bright told them later. 'These are the last islands on our journey. After this, we're going to America. I'll take you there with us.'

◆

So how did the five men feel when they left their beautiful island? They were, of course, happy because they weren't prisoners. Cyrus and Spillet were ready. There was work for them in the new world outside the island. They wanted to marry and have families. And Spillet wanted to tell the world their story.

Nab and Top only wanted to follow their master.

Pencroft wanted a life at sea. And now he could tell one or two new stories.

Herbert was now a young man. Two years on a Pacific island was very exciting, but he wanted to see his family again. And he too wanted to start a new life in the outside world.

'What would you like to do, Herbert?' Cyrus Smith asked him on the ship. They could see America now.

'I'd like to be the captain of a ship.'

ACTIVITIES

Chapters 1–4

Before you read

1 Read the Introduction to this book. What will happen in the story? What do you think?

2 Find these words in your dictionary. They are all in the story.

balloon bark (v) bow (n) branch cave island land (n) master match mysterious prisoner rock rope sign wave (n)

 a Which words are for people?
 b Which things can you climb?
 c What can you walk on?
 d What can you fly in?
 e What can you go into?
 f What can you swim in?
 g What gives you light?
 h What comes from a tree?
 i What does a dog do?
 j What can you use when you kill small animals?
 k Which word means 'strange'?
 l What tells you that something is there?

After you read

3 Answer these questions.

 a The men in the balloon want to go north. Where does the balloon take them?
 b Why do they throw everything out of the balloon?
 c What do you eat on the island?
 d What mysterious things happen?

4 Work with two other students. You are in a balloon. It is going down. One person has to jump or you will all die. Think of a job. Tell the other people about your job. Why is it more important than their job? Who will jump?

Chapters 5–9

Before you read

5 You are going to a Pacific island. You are the first person on the island. You can only take three things with you. What will you take? You can only take two other people with you. Who will you take?

6 Find the words *pirate* and *torpedo* in your dictionary. What are they in your language?

After you read

7 Why are these important to the story?
   a matches
   b rope
   c branches
   d Cave House

8 What do you know about the island and the things on it? Talk about them.

Chapters 10–13

Before you read

9 Who or what is helping the five men? What do you think?

10 Find these words in your dictionary. Then answer the questions.
   captain   prince   submarine
   Which:
   a never goes on land?
   b is important on a ship?
   c is important in a country?

After you read

11 Who says or writes these words?
   a 'Now *I* am dying.'
   b 'Him! But isn't he dead?'
   c 'I know that this is your submarine.'
   d 'I hated the British.'
   e 'These are the last islands on our journey.'
   f 'I'd like to be the captain of a ship.'

Writing

12 Write Spillet's story for the *New York Herald*.

13 Write Herbert's first letter to his parents after he arrives in America.

14 Write about a day in the life of Captain Nemo, in his cave.

15 Write a short story. Start with these words:

One day I found a big box on the beach. In it there was/were . . .

What things were in the box? How did you use them?

Answers for the Activities in this book are published in our free resource packs for teachers, the Penguin Readers Factsheets, or available on a separate sheet. Please write to your local Pearson Education office or to: Marketing Department, Penguin Longman Publishing, 5 Bentinck Street, London W1M 5RN.